bridges to contemplative living
with thomas merton

seven:
adjusting your life's vision

edited by jonathan montaldo & robert g. toth
of the merton institute for contemplative living

ave maria press AMP notre dame, indiana

Ave Maria Press gratefully acknowledges the permission of the following publishers for use of excerpts from these books:

Conjectures of a Guilty Bystander by Thomas Merton, copyright © 1966 by the Abbey of Gethsemani. Used by permission of Doubleday, a division of Random House, Inc.

Dancing in the Water of Life: The Journals of Thomas Merton, Volume Five 1963–1965 by Thomas Merton and edited by Robert E. Daggy, copyright © 1997 by The Merton Legacy Trust. Reprinted by permission of HarperCollins Publishers.

Honorable Reader: Reflections on My Work by Thomas Merton, copyright © 1989 by The Merton Legacy Trust. Used with permission.

"A Letter to Pablo Antonio Cuadra Concerning Giants." From *The Collected Poems of Thomas Merton*, copyright © 1963 by The Abbey of Gethsemani. Reprinted by permission of New Directions Publishing Corp.

On Pilgrimage, by Dorothy Day, copyright © 1999 by William B. Eerdmans Publishing Company. Reprinted with permission of the publisher.

The Psalms: An Inclusive Language Version Based on the Grail Translation from the Hebrew. Published through exclusive license agreement by G.I.A. Publications, Inc. Copyright © 1963, 1986 by The Grail (England). Used by permission of G.I.A.

Seeing with the Eyes of Love: On the Imitation of Christ, by Eknath Easwaran, founder of the Blue Mountain Center of Meditation, 2nd Edition, copyright © 1996; reprinted by permission of Nilgiri Press.

Shambhala: The Sacred Path of the Warrior by Chögyam Trungpa, copyright © 1988. Reprinted by arrangement with Shambhala Publications, Inc.

The Silent Cry: Mysticism and Resistance, by Dorothee Soelle, copyright © 2001 by Fortress Press. Reprinted by permission of Augsburg Fortress Publishers.

The Soul of Rumi: A New Collection of Ecstatic Songs edited by Coleman Barks, copyright © 2001 by HarperCollins Publishers. Reprinted by permission of HarperCollins Publishers.

Thomas Merton in Alaska, copyright © 1988, 1989 by The Trustees of the Merton Legacy Trust. Reprinted by permission of New Directions Publishing Corp.

Founded in 1865, Ave Maria Press is a ministry of the Indiana Province of Holy Cross.

www.avemariapress.com

ISBN-10 1-59471-240-9   ISBN-13 978-1-59471-240-1

Cover and text design by Andy Wagoner.

Cover photograph © Robert Hill Photography.

Interior photograph; Alaska, by Thomas Merton. Used with permission of the Merton Legacy Trust and the Thomas Merton Center at Bellarmine University. Interior photograph of Thomas Merton on p. 7 by John Lyons. Used with permission of the Merton Legacy Trust.

Printed and bound in the United States of America.

I stand among you as one who offers a small message of hope that first, there are always people who dare to seek on the margin of society, who are not dependent on social acceptance, not dependent on social routine, and prefer a kind of free-floating existence under a state of risk. And among these people, if they are faithful to their own calling, to their own vocation, and to their own message from God, communication on the deepest level is possible. And the deepest level of communication is not communication, but communion. It is wordless. It is beyond words, and it is beyond speech, and it is beyond concept. Not that we discover a new unity. We discover an older unity. We are already one. But we imagine that we are not. And what we have to recover is our original unity. What we have to be is what we are.

THOMAS MERTON
The Asian Journal of Thomas Merton

A NOTE ABOUT INCLUSIVE LANGUAGE
Thomas Merton wrote at a time before inclusive language was common practice. In light of his inclusive position on so many issues and his references to our essential unity, we hope these texts will be read from an inclusive point of view.

CONTENTS

Introduction   6

  What do we mean by contemplative living?

  Who Was Thomas Merton?

  Using Bridges to Contemplative Living with Thomas
  Merton

  What do we mean by contemplative dialogue?

  Eight Principles for Entering into Contemplative Dialogue

  Additional Resources

Session 1: Becoming Instruments of Reconciliation   15

Session 2: Nonviolence: A Vision of Hope
            for Humankind   20

Session 3: A Prophetic, Radically Catholic,
            Contemplative Vision   25

Session 4: Listening for God in the Voice of
            the Stranger   30

Session 5: Our Vocation to Unity   35

Session 6: Voicing Our Inner "Yes" to God
            and Neighbor   40

Session 7: Finding Our Place in God's Scheme
            of Things   45

Session 8: Dying as a Catalyst for Continuing
            Transformation   50

Concluding Meditations   55

Sources   57

Another Voice: Biographical Sketches   60

Introduction

What do we mean by contemplative living?

Life is a spiritual journey. Contemplative living is a way of responding to our everyday experiences by consciously attending to our relationships. It deepens our awareness of our connectedness and communion with others, becomes a positive force of change in our lives, and provides meaningful direction to our journey. Ultimately, contemplative living leads us to a sense of well-being, profound gratitude, and a clearer understanding of our purpose in life.

Living contemplatively begins with ourselves but leads us in the end to embrace deeply not only our truest self, but God, neighbor, and all of creation. By reflecting on our everyday experiences, we seek the depths of our inner truth. By exploring our beliefs, illusions, attitudes, and assumptions, we find our true self and discover how we relate to the larger community. Contemplative living directs our minds and hearts to the truly important issues of human existence, making us less likely to be captivated by the superficial distractions that so easily occupy our time.

Who was Thomas Merton?

For over sixty years, the thought and writings of Thomas Merton have guided spiritual seekers across the world. His writings offer important insights into four essential relationships—with self, with God, with other people, and with all of creation. While the

Christian tradition is the foundation of his perspective, he is open and inclusive in his examination of other religious traditions, recognizing the important contribution of all faith traditions to the history of civilization. He drew from their strengths to enhance the spiritual growth of individuals and communities.

Thomas Merton was born in Prades, France, in 1915. His mother was from the United States and his father from New Zealand. Educated in France, England, and the United States, he received a master's degree in English from Columbia University. In 1938 he was baptized into the Catholic Church. He taught at St. Bonaventure University for a year and then in 1941 entered the Cistercian Order as a monk of the Abbey of Gethsemani in Kentucky. Directed by his Abbot, Dom Frederic Dunne, Merton wrote his autobiography, *The Seven Storey Mountain*, which was published in 1948.

For fifteen years he served as Master of Scholastics and Novices while writing many books and articles on the spiritual life, interreligious understanding, peace, and social justice issues. In December of 1968, he journeyed to Asia to attend a conference of contemplatives near Bangkok, Thailand. While there he was accidentally electrocuted and died at the age of fifty-three.

Interest in Merton has grown steadily since his death. *The Seven Storey Mountain,* which appears on lists of the one hundred most important books of the last century, has been in print ever since its first edition and has sold millions of copies. The volume of printed work by and about him attests to Merton's popularity. His works have been translated into thirty-five languages and new foreign language editions continue to be printed. The International Thomas Merton Society currently has thirty chapters in the United States and fourteen in other countries.

Thomas Merton is distinguished among contemporary spiritual writers by the depth and substance of his thinking. Merton was a scholar who distilled the best thinking of the best theologians, philosophers, and poets throughout the centuries, from both the West and the East, and presented their ideas in the context of the Christian worldview. His remarkable and enduring popularity indicates that his work continues to speak to the minds and hearts of people searching for answers to life's important questions. For many he is a spiritual guide, and for others he offers a place to retreat to in difficult times. His writings take people into deep places within themselves and offer insight into the paradoxes of life. Merton struggled to be contemplative in a world of action, yet he offered no quick fix or "Ten Easy Steps" to a successful spiritual life.

USING BRIDGES TO CONTEMPLATIVE LIVING WITH THOMAS MERTON

Bridges is intended for anyone seeking to live more contemplatively. For some it initiates a spiritual journey, for others it leads to re-examination or recovery of a neglected spiritual life, and for still others it deepens an already vibrant spirituality. Through reflection and dialogue on specific spiritual themes, participants revisit and refresh their perspectives on and understanding of life. They explore the strength and balance of the relationships that ultimately determine who they are: relationships with self, God, others, and nature. Through examining these relationships, participants probe their understanding of life's great questions:

"Who am I?"
"Who is God?"
"Why am I here?"
"What am I to do with my life?"

The selected readings move participants in and out of four dimensions of contemplative living— *Awakening* to an ever-deepening awareness of "true-self"; *Contemplation* of a life experienced from a God-centered perspective; *Compassion* in relationships with others; and *Unity* realized in our undeniable and essential interconnectedness with all of creation. This fourfold process of spiritual formation frames much of Merton's thought and writing.

This is not a spiritual formation program in some "otherworldly" sense. Merton insisted that our spiritual life is our everyday lived experience. There is no separation between them. Bridges does not require an academic background in theology, religion, or spirituality, nor does it require the use of any particular spiritual practices or prayers. There are no levels of perfection, goals to attain, or measurements of progress. This is not an academic or scholarly undertaking. Everyone will find a particular way of contemplative living within his or her own circumstances, religious tradition, and spiritual practices.

The Bridges to Contemplative Living with Thomas Merton series is especially designed for small group dialogue. The selected themes of each session are intended to progressively inform and deepen the relationships that form our everyday lives. Each session begins with scripture and ends in prayer. In between there are time and mental space for spiritual reading, reflection, and contemplative dialogue.

What do we mean by contemplative dialogue?

Contemplative dialogue is meant to be non-threatening, a "safe place" for open sharing and discussion. It is not outcome-oriented. It's not even about fully understanding or comprehending what one reads or hears from the other participants. The focus is on *listening* rather than formulating a response to what another is saying. Simply hearing and accepting another's point of view and reflecting on it can inform and enlighten our own perspective in a way that debating or analyzing it cannot. The pace of conversation is slower in contemplative dialogue than in most other conversations. We are challenged to listen more carefully and approach different points of view by looking at the deeper values and issues underlying them.

Eight Principles for Entering into Contemplative Dialogue

1. Keep in mind that Bridges focuses on our "lived experience" and how the session theme connects to everyday life. Keep your comments rooted in your own experience and refrain from remarks that are overly abstract, philosophical, or theoretical.

2. Express your own thoughts knowing that others will listen and reflect upon what you say. It is helpful to use "I" statements like "I believe . . ." or "I am confused by that response." Try framing your remarks with phrases such as "My assumption is that . . ." or "My experience has been . . ." While others in the group may very well not respond to your thoughts verbally, trust that they are hearing you.

3. Pay attention to the assumptions, attitudes, and experiences underlying your initial or surface thoughts on the topic. Ask yourself questions like: "Why am I drawn to this particular part of the reading?" "What makes me feel this way?"

4. Remember to listen first and refrain from thinking about how you might respond to another's comments. Simply listen to and accept his or her thoughts on the subject without trying to challenge, critique, or even respond aloud to them.

5. Trust the group. Observe how the participants' ideas, reflections, common concerns, assumptions, and attitudes come together and form a collective group mind.

6. Reflect before speaking and be concise. Make one point or relate one experience, then stop and allow others to do the same.

7. Expect periods of silence during the dialogue. Learn to be comfortable with the silence and resist the urge to speak just because there is silence.

8. Avoid cross-talking. In time you will adjust to saying something and not receiving a response and to listening without asking a question, challenging, or responding directly. Simply speaking to the theme or idea from your own experience or perspective takes some practice. Be patient with yourself and the other members of your group and watch for deepening levels of dialogue.

These principles for contemplative dialogue are extracted from the work of the Centre for Contemplative Dialogue. For more complete information visit www .contemplativedialogue.org.

ADDITIONAL RESOURCES

A leader's guide and introductory DVD for the Bridges series are available from Ave Maria Press.

Online resources available at www.avemariapress .com include:

- Leader's Guide
- Sample pages
- Suggested Retreat Schedule
- Program Evaluation Form
- Links to other books about Thomas Merton
- Interview with Robert Toth of the Merton Institute for Contemplative Living

FROM THE MERTON INSTITUTE FOR CONTEMPLATIVE LIVING: WWW.MERTONINSTITUTE.ORG

Merton: A Film Biography (1 hour) provides an excellent overview on Merton's life and spiritual journey.

Soul Searching: The Journey of Thomas Merton is a sixty-seven-minute DVD that goes to the heart of Merton's spiritual journey through the perspective of Merton's friends, Merton scholars, and authorities on the spiritual life.

Contemplation and Action is a periodic newsletter from the Merton Institute with information about new Merton publications, programs, and events. It is free and can be obtained by visiting the institute's website or calling 1-800-886-7275.

The Thomas Merton Spiritual Development Program is a basic introduction to Merton's life and his insights on contemplative spirituality, social justice, and inter-religious dialogue. Especially designed for youth, it includes a participant's workbook/journal.

Weekly Merton Reflections: Receive a brief reflection from Merton's works via e-mail each week by registering at www.mertoninstitute.org or by contacting:

The Merton Institute for Contemplative Living
2117 Payne Street
Louisville, KY 40206
1-800-886-7275

session one
BECOMING INSTRUMENTS OF RECONCILIATION

OPENING REFLECTION

PSALM 16:3–6

He has put into my heart a marvelous love
for the faithful ones who dwell in his land.
Those who choose other gods increase their
sorrows.
Never will I offer their offerings of blood.
Never will I take their name upon my lips.

O Lord, it is you who are my portion and cup;
it is you yourself who are my prize.
The lot marked out for me is my delight:
welcome indeed the heritage that falls to me!

INTRODUCTION TO THE TEXTS

In the ceremony that marked Merton's reception as a
novice at Gethsemani, when he exchanged his street
clothes for a white robe in the presence of the monastic community, his Abbot, Frederic Dunne asked him
a ritual question in Latin: "*Quid petis*?" [What are you
seeking?] Merton responded with the novice's ritual
answer: "The mercy of God and of this Order." The
novice did not ask for perfection in virtues, mystical
experiences, or peace of mind. He asked instead for
God's compassion and loving kindness that would be
mediated to him every day by his community's con-
tinued acceptance of him just as he was. Being thus

received into his community's "school of charity," as Saint Bernard of Clairvaux called it, Merton experienced his community's first formal lesson in the long course of becoming an instrument of mercy for his community and for the world.

Francis of Assisi prayed to be an instrument of God's peace. Where there was hatred, he sought to sow love. In valleys of sadness, he prayed to sow joy. In gardens of despair, he sought to seed hope. The love and compassion that saves the world begins as a seed that grows to a rich harvest by ongoing decisions to serve others. Our decision to live contemplatively only comes to harvest through fertilizing deeds. Perhaps we should fast and go hungry from words like "compassion" for it is only *deeds* of compassion that matter, only *acts* of forgiving and accepting one another that makes community a reality. Deeds of merciful reconciliation plant peace in our world.

MERTON'S VOICE
FROM *HONORABLE READER*

It is true, political problems are not solved by love and mercy. But the world of politics is not the only world, and unless political decisions rest on a foundation of something better and higher than politics, they can never do any real good for me. When a country has to be rebuilt after war, the passions and energies of war are no longer enough. There must be a new force, the power of love, the power of understanding and human compassion, the strength of selflessness and cooperation, as the creative dynamism of the will to live and to build, and the will to forgive. The will for reconciliation.

The principles given in this book are simple and more or less traditional. They are the principles derived from religious wisdom, which, in the present case, is Christian. But many of these principles run parallel to the ancient teachings of Buddhism. They are in fact in large part universal truths. They are truths upon which, for centuries, man has slowly and with difficulty built a civilized world in the effort to make happiness possible, not merely by making life materially better, but by helping men to understand and live their lives more fruitfully.

The key to this understanding is the truth that "No man is an island." A selfish life cannot be fruitful. It cannot be true. It contradicts the very nature of man. The dire effect of this contradiction cannot be avoided; where men live selfishly, in quest of brute power and lust and money, they destroy one another. The only way to change such a world is to change the thoughts and desires of the men who live in it. The conditions of our world are simply an outward expression of our thoughts and desires. . . .

We must all believe in love and in peace. We must believe in the power of love. We must recognize that our being itself is grounded in love; that is to say, that we come into being because we are loved and because we are meant to love others. The failure to believe this and to live accordingly creates instead a deep mistrust, a suspicion of others, a hatred of others, a failure to love. When a man attempts to live by and for himself alone, he becomes a little "island" of hate, greed, suspicion, fear, desire. Then his whole outlook on life is falsified. All his judgments are affected by that untruth. In order to recover the true perspective, which is that of love and compassion, he must once again learn, in simplicity, truth, and peace, that "No man is an island." (pp. 125–126)

ANOTHER VOICE
DOROTHY DAY, *ON PILGRIMAGE*

Whenever I groan within myself and think how hard it is to keep writing about love in these times of tension and strife, which may at any moment become for us all a time of terror, I think to myself, "What else is the world interested in?" What else do we all want, each one of us, except to love and be loved, in our families, in our work, in all our relationships? God is Love. Love casts out fear. Even the most ardent revolutionist, seeking to change the world, to overturn the tables of the moneychangers, is trying to make a world where it is easier for people to love, to stand in that relationship to each other. We want with all our hearts to love, to be loved. And not just in the family but to look upon all as our mothers, sisters, brothers, children. It is when we love the most intensely and most humanly that we can recognize how tepid is our love for others. . . .

When you love people, you see all the good in them, all the Christ in them. God sees Christ, His Son, in us and loves us. And so we should see Christ in others, and nothing else, and love them. There can never be enough of it. There can never be enough thinking about it. St. John of the Cross said that where there was no love, put love and you would take out love. . . .

It is an easy thing to talk about love, but it is something to be proven, to be suffered, to be learned. (pp. 123–125)

18

Reflect and Dialogue

What images, words, or sentences in the readings most resonate with your life's experiences? In what ways do they connect with your life?

What have you learned about the kind of love that sustains peaceful relationships?

What is your personal prescription for healing divisions among us? Are you taking it yourself?

For what are you really hoping when you pray for peace?

Closing

Conclude with one of the meditations on pages 55–56 or with a period of quiet reflection.

session two

NONVIOLENCE: A VISION OF HOPE FOR HUMANKIND

OPENING REFLECTION

PSALM 17:4B–5, 15

I kept from violence because of your word,
I kept my feet firmly in your paths;
there was no faltering in my steps.

As for me, in my justice I shall see your face
and be filled, when I awake,
with the sight of your glory.

INTRODUCTION TO THE TEXTS

Being nonviolent in our relationships is the surest indicator that we are all potentially loving and compassionate human beings. Nonviolence in our actions, in the way we speak and even in the conscious flow of our thoughts and emotions is a preeminent sign that at the core of our humanness is a capacity to bear the presence of the Holy Spirit.

During secondary school in England, Merton wrote a paper in support of Mohandas Gandhi's nonviolent resistance to the British occupation of India. Much later at Gethsemani he published a small collection of Gandhi's writings under the title *Gandhi and Nonviolence*. Merton's insistence that his Christian vocation required that he practice nonviolence in thought, word, and deed was foundational to his understanding of what it meant to be a contemplative. In one of his most beautiful essays, "Blessed Are The Meek," Merton argued that no Christian can ultimately despair of humanity. In spite of evidence to the contrary, we are to persevere humbly in hope. We are to renounce violence and strive to accept every sister and brother as part of the eternal community that we shall know fully only at our life's end when we are received into the community of God's Love prepared for all from the beginning of the world (*The Gospel of Epiphanius*).

MERTON'S VOICE
FROM "BLESSED ARE THE MEEK: THE CHRISTIAN ROOTS OF NONVIOLENCE"

Christian hope and Christian humility are inseparable. The quality of nonviolence is decided largely by the purity of the Christian hope behind it. In its insistence on certain human values, the Second Vatican Council, following *Pacem in Terris*, displayed a basically optimistic trust in man himself. Not that there is not wickedness in the world, but today trust in God cannot be completely divorced from a certain trust in man. The Christian knows that there are radically sound possibilities in every man, and he believes that love and grace always have the power to bring out those possibilities at the most unexpected moments. Therefore if he has hopes that God will grant peace to the world it is because he also trusts that man, God's creature, is not basically evil: that there is in man a potentiality for peace and order which can be realized provided the right conditions are there. The Christian will do his part in creating these conditions by preferring love and trust to hate and suspiciousness. Obviously, once again, this "hope in man" must not be naïve. . . .

It is therefore very important to understand that Christian humility implies not only a certain wise reserve in regard to one's own judgments—a good sense which sees that we are not always necessarily infallible in our ideas—but it also cherishes positive and trustful expectations of others. . . .

In summary, the meekness and humility—which Christ extolled in the Sermon on the Mount and which are the bases of true Christian nonviolence—are inseparable from an eschatological Christian hope which is completely open to the presence of God in the world and therefore to the presence of our brother and sister who is always seen, no matter who they may be, in the perspectives of the Kingdom. Despair is not permitted to the meek, the humble, the afflicted, the ones famished for justice, the merciful, the clean of heart, and the peacemakers. All the beatitudes "hope against hope," bear everything, believe everything, hope for everything, endure everything" (1 Corinthians 13:7). The beatitudes are simply aspects of love. They refuse to despair of the world and abandon it to a supposedly evil fate that it has brought upon itself. Instead, like Christ himself, the Christian takes upon his own shoulders the yoke of the Savior, meek and humble of heart. This yoke is the burden of the world's sin with all its confusions, and all its problems. These sins, confusions and problems are our very own. We do not disown them. (pp. 257–258)

ANOTHER VOICE
MOHANDAS GANDHI, *ESSENTIAL WRITINGS*

If one does not practice nonviolence in one's personal relations with others and hopes to use it in bigger affairs, one is vastly mistaken. Nonviolence, like charity, must begin at home. But if it is necessary for the individual to be trained in nonviolence, it is even more necessary for the nation to be trained likewise. One cannot be nonviolent in one's own circle and violent outside it. Or else, one is not truly nonviolent in one's own circle; often the nonviolence is only in appearance. . . .

If one has pride and egoism, there is no nonviolence. Nonviolence is not possible without humility. My own experience is that, whenever I have acted nonviolently, I have been led to it and sustained by the higher promptings of an unseen Power. Through my own will I should have miserably failed. . . .

Nonviolence is a very slow process, you will perhaps say. Yes, possibly, under the existing adverse circumstances to begin with. But it will gather momentum and speed in an incalculable manner as you proceed. I am an irrepressible optimist. My optimism rests on my belief in the infinite possibilities of the individual to develop nonviolence. The more you develop it in your own being, the more infectious it becomes till it overwhelms your surroundings and by and by might over-sweep the world.

Nonviolence succeeds only when we have a living faith in God. Buddha, Jesus, Mohammed—they were all warriors of peace in their own style. We have to enrich the heritage left by these world teachers. God has God's own wonderful way of executing God's plans and choosing God's instruments. All the world teachers, you should know, began with a zero! (pp. 123–124)

Reflect and Dialogue

What images, words, or sentences in the readings most resonate with your life's experiences? In what ways do they connect with your life?

Who in your life has most witnessed for you a "nonviolent alternative" to human problems?

How would you coach a person younger than you to act nonviolently in both word and deed?

In what ways do you honestly know that your nonviolence has limits?

Closing

Conclude with one of the meditations on pages 55–56 or with a period of quiet reflection.

session three

A PROPHETIC, RADICALLY CATHOLIC, CONTEMPLATIVE VISION

OPENING REFLECTION

PSALM 19:2–5

The heavens proclaim the glory of God
and the firmament shows forth the work
of his hands.

Day unto day takes up the story
and night unto night makes known the
message.

No speech, no word, no voice is heard
yet their span extends through all the earth,
their words to the utmost bounds of the
world.

INTRODUCTION TO THE TEXTS

A more expansive vision of life is the work of training and grace. Contemplatives view everything through a wide-open lens. The contemplative mind's eye opens to include everything in God's "hidden ground of love." Possessed by a spirit of inclusiveness, a contemplative heart is hospitable to every stranger. Albert Einstein urged our charity to be coextensive with the circumference of the universe. Those who discipline their hearts to expand beyond the horizons of their personal interests are accorded the gifts of our humanity's deeper potential.

25

Merton's inner work was a life-long effort to "uncage his mind," as Robert Woodward once said about Merton in *Newsweek Magazine*. Every effort by human beings to seek God attracted Merton's studious attention. His mind was free of absolutist theories about how one should love God and neighbor. By his studies, his prayers, and his daily practice, Merton disciplined his heart to make himself pliable for the grace that would make him free to serve others.

> If I can unite in myself, in my own spiritual life, the thought of the East and the West, of the Greek and Latin Fathers, I will create in myself the reunion of the divided Church, and from that unity in myself can come the exterior and visible unity of the Church. For, if we want to bring together East and West, we cannot do it by imposing one upon the other. We must contain both in ourselves and transcend them both in Christ.
>
> —*A Search for Solitude*, p. 87

MERTON'S VOICE
FROM *HONORABLE READER*

In the silence of the countryside and the forest, in the cloistered solitude of my monastery, I have discovered the whole Western Hemisphere. Here I have been able, though the grace of God, to explore the New World. . . .

It seems that I have heard the voice of all the hemisphere in the silence of my monastery, a voice that speaks from the depths of my being with a clarity at once magnificent and terrible: as if I had in my heart the vast and solitary pampas, the brilliant hoarfrost of the Bolivian plateau, the thin air of the terraced valleys of the Incas, the splendor and suavity of Quito, the cold plains of Bogatá, and the mysterious jungles of the Amazon. . . . It seems that the unending beauty of the New World with its limitless possibilities moves within me like a giant sleeper in whose presence I am unable to remain indifferent. In reality, it seems at times that this presence inside me speaks with the voice of God Himself; and I struggle vainly to grasp and to understand some word, some syllable of the destiny of the New World—the destiny that is still hidden in the mystery of Providence.

One thing I know—that it is my destiny to be a contemplative, a Christian, and an American. I can satisfy my vocation with nothing that is partial or provincial. . . .

I cannot be a partial American and I cannot be, which is even sadder, a partial Catholic. For me Catholicism is not confined to one culture, one nation, one age, one race. My faith is not a mixture of the Irish Catholicism of the United States and the splendid and vital Catholicism, reborn during the last war, of my native France. Though I admire the cathedrals and the past of Catholicism in Latin America, my Catholicism goes beyond the Spanish tradition. I cannot believe that Catholicism is tied to the destinies of any group which confusedly expresses the economic illusions of a social class. . . . My Catholicism is all the world and all ages. It dates from the beginning of the world. The first man was the image of Christ and contained Christ, even as he was created, as savior in his heart. The first man was destined to be the ancestor of his Redeemer and the first woman was the mother of all life, in the image of the Immaculate Daughter who was full of grace, Mother of mercy, Mother of the saved. (pp. 40–41)

ANOTHER VOICE
EDITH STEIN, *THE MYSTERY OF CHRISTMAS*

One with God. . . . If Christ is the Head and we the members in the Mystical Body, then we relate to each other as member to member and we are all one in God, a divine life. If God is in us and if he is love, then it cannot be otherwise but to love one another. Therefore, our love for our brothers and sisters is the measure of our love for God. But it is different from a natural, human love which affects this one or that who may be related to us, or who may be close to us because of the bonds of temperament or common interests. The rest are "strangers" who don't concern us, perhaps even by their presence annoy us, so that love is kept as far away as possible. For the Christian there is no "strange human being." He is in every instance the "neighbor" whom we have with us and who is most in need of us. It makes no difference whether he is related or not, whether we "like" him or not, whether he is "morally worthy" of help or not. The love of Christ knows no bounds, it never ceases, it never withdraws in the face of hatred or foul play. He came for the sake of sinners and not for the righteous. If the love of Christ lives in us, then we do as he did and seek after the lost sheep. (pp. 12–13)

Reflect and Dialogue

What images, words, or sentences in the readings most resonate with your life's experiences? In what ways do they connect with your life?

How wide are your religious affiliations?

Who are your life's strangers—the people who don't concern you?

What keeps you caged in the gated communities of your provincial interests?

Closing

Conclude with one of the meditations on pages 55–56 or with a period of quiet reflection.

session four
LISTENING FOR GOD IN THE VOICE OF THE STRANGER

OPENING REFLECTION
PSALM 148:7–8, 11–13

> Praise the Lord from the earth,
> sea creatures and all oceans,
> fire and hail, snow and mist,
> stormy winds that obey his word;
>
> All earth's kings and peoples,
> earth's princes and rulers;
> young men and maidens,
> old men together with children.
>
> Let them praise the name of the Lord
> for he alone is exalted.
> The splendor of his name
> reaches beyond heaven and earth.

INTRODUCTION TO THE TEXTS

In Saint Benedict's *Rule* for monks, all are enjoined to receive guests to the monastery as if Christ were arriving at the gate. Monks train to personify hospitality. Excluding no one from a reverent greeting, monks listen for the "word" that a particular guest is bringing for his own and his community's salvation.

As we practice contemplative dialogue, our collective voices can become strange to our ears, especially when our dialogue partners speak their own truths unchecked by moralizing theories. Contemplative dialogue allows everyone to take the risk of voicing something new. We are practicing radical hospitality as we listen carefully to the "strange voices" among us, even when the strange voice is our own.

Merton's letter writing was gracious and voluminous to persons of every status. His letters reveal his full engagement with the monk's task of being hospitable to the presence of Christ in all. His contacts with those who did not share his religious traditions were grounded in catholic hospitality and reverence for the person. Hospitality is the great virtue that expands the horizons of our hearts when we choose to live contemplatively.

MERTON'S VOICE
FROM "A LETTER TO PABLO ANTONIO CUADRA CONCERNING GIANTS"

It is my belief that we should not be too sure of having found Christ in ourselves until we have found him also in the part of humanity that is most remote from our own.

Christ is found not in loud and pompous declarations but in humble and fraternal dialogue. He is found less in a truth that is imposed than in a truth that is shared. . . .

If I insist on giving you my truth, and never stop to receive your truth in return, then there can be no truth between us. Christ is present "where two or three are gathered in my name." But to be gathered in the name

31

of Christ is to be gathered in the name of the Word made flesh. . . .

God speaks, and God is to be heard, not only on Sinai, not only in my own heart, but in the voice of the stranger. That is why the peoples of the Orient, and all primitive peoples in general, make so much of the mystery of hospitality.

God must be allowed to speak unpredictably. The Holy Spirit, the very voice of Divine Liberty, must always be like the wind in "blowing where he pleases" (John 3:8). In the mystery of the Old Testament there was already a tension between the Law and the Prophets. In the New Testament the Spirit is the new Law, and he is everywhere. He certainly inspires and protects the visible Church, but if we cannot see him unexpectedly in the stranger and the alien, we will not understand him even in the Church. We must find him in our enemy, or we may lose him even in our friend. We must find him in the pagan, or we will lose him in ourselves, substituting for his living presence an empty abstraction. How can we reveal to others what we cannot discover in them ourselves? We must, then, see the truth in the stranger, and the truth we see must be a newly living truth, not just a projection of a dead and conventional idea of our own—a projection of our own self upon the stranger. (pp. 382–385)

ANOTHER VOICE
EKNATH EASWARAN, *SEEING WITH THE EYES OF LOVE*

Eden, to me, is not a place at all. It is a state of consciousness—that state in which we transcend our physical separateness and become aware of the divine ground of existence within. That is our native state, the place where we really belong. Saint Francis is not Francis of Assisi; he is Francis of Eden. Saint Teresa is not Teresa of Avila; she is Teresa of Eden. They carry Eden around with them. That is why they are at home everywhere, and like superb hosts and hostesses, they want nothing more than for the rest of us to be at home there too. . . .

In Hinduism we have an ancient mythic counter-point to the Fall, and it is very much in harmony with the Big Bang theory too. In the beginning, according to this myth, there was only consciousness: a vast cosmic egg full of unitive awareness. Inexplicably, in a creative burst of differentiation, this cosmic egg exploded in a thousand directions. You and I and all the rest of life are each tiny fragments of that original unity—infinitesimal bits of a vast jigsaw puzzle. Each of us carries with us a tiny bit of the cosmic yolk, a fragment of the divine. And it's that dab of yolk in all of us—the memory of unitive consciousness—that keeps us from ever being fully at home in a world of separateness.

Thomas Merton describes this infinitesimal bit of divine yolk in haunting language:

> At the center of our being is a point of nothingness which is untouched by sin and by illusion, a point of pure truth, a point or spark which belongs entirely to God, which is never at our disposal, from which God disposes of our lives, which is inaccessible to the fantasies of our mind or to the brutalities of our will.
>
> —*Conjectures of A Guilty Bystander*,
> p. 158

It is this still point which enables us to work tirelessly for the welfare of all, and which draws us inward in the long return to our native state of being. (pp. 128, 130)

REFLECT AND DIALOGUE

What images, words, or sentences in the readings most resonate with your life's experiences? In what ways do they connect with your life?

How does hospitality play a role in your spiritual living?

Toward what types or classes of people are you least hospitable?

Who turned your life around by showing you hospitality just when you most needed to be graciously received?

CLOSING

Conclude with one of the meditations on pages 55–56 or with a period of quiet reflection.

session five
OUR VOCATION
TO UNITY

OPENING REFLECTION

PSALM 87:4–5

> Babylon and Egypt I will count
> among those who know me;
> Philistia, Tyre, Ethiopia,
> these will be her children
> and Zion shall be called "Mother"
> for all shall be her children.

INTRODUCTION TO THE TEXTS

Contemplative living is the continuing process of integrating our personal experiences into a one-pointed search for God with and through our neighbors. Contemplative living is not just another compartment of experience separate from the other compartments into which we segment aspects of daily living. In his book *The Inner Experience,* Merton defined contemplative living as a life that seeks unity.

> The first thing that you have to do, before you even start thinking about such a thing as contemplation, is to try to recover your basic natural unity, to reintegrate your compartmentalized being into a coordinated and simple whole and learn to live as a unified human person. This means that you have to

bring back together the fragments of your distracted existence so that when you say "I," there is really someone present to support the pronoun you have uttered. (pp. 3-4)

By means of various practices and techniques, contemplatives use any right actions that will enhance their conscious—and gradually even unconscious—awareness that they are present to God and God is present to them through all their experiences.

Merton's Voice
From *Honorable Reader*

The contemplative life applies wherever there is life. Wherever man and society exist; where there are hopes, ideals, aspirations for a better future; where there is love—and where there is mingled pain and happiness—there the contemplative life has a place, because life, happiness, pain, ideals, aspirations, work, art, and other things have significance. If these things have no significance, why waste our time on them? But, if they have significance, then the independent significance of each must converge in some way into a central and universal significance, which comes from a hidden reality. This central reality has to be a "catholic" reality, a "divine" reality. The reality central to my life is the life of God. To know this is the contemplative's objective.

In my case, the word of salvation, the gospel of Jesus Christ, has led me to solitude and silence. My vocation is rare, perhaps, but contemplation does not exist only within the walls of the cloister. Every man, to live a life full of significance, is called simply to know the significant interior of life and to find ultimate significance in its proper inscrutable existence, in spite of himself, in spite of the world and appearances, in the Living God. Every man born on this earth is called to find and realize himself in Christ and, through Him, to comprehend the unity of Christ with all men, so much so that he loves them as they love themselves and is one with them almost as he is one with himself: then the spirit of Christ is one with those who love him. (pp. 39–40)

ANOTHER VOICE
CHÖGYAM TRUNGPA, *SHAMBHALA: THE SACRED PATH OF THE WARRIOR*

The key to warriorship and the first principle of Shambhala vision is not being afraid of who you are. Ultimately, that is the definition of bravery: not being afraid of yourself. Shambhala vision teaches that, in the face of the world's great problems, we can be heroic and kind at the same time. Shambhala vision is the opposite of selfishness. When we are afraid of ourselves, and afraid of the seeming threat the world presents, then we become extremely selfish. We want to build our own little nests, our own cocoons, so that we can live by ourselves in a secure way.

But we can be much more than that. We must try to think beyond our homes, beyond the fire burning in the fireplace, beyond sending our children to school or getting to work in the morning. We must try to think how we can help this world. If we don't help, nobody will. It is our turn to help the world. At the same time, helping others does not mean abandoning our individual lives. You don't have to rush out and become the mayor of your city or the president of the United States in order to help others, but you can begin with your relatives and friends and the people around you. In fact, you can start with yourself. The important point to realize is that you are never off duty. You can never just relax, because the whole world needs help.

. . . The premise of Shambhala vision is that, in order to establish an enlightened society for others, we need to discover what inherently we have to offer the world. So, to begin with, we should make an effort to examine our own experience, in order to see what it contains that is of value in helping ourselves and others to uplift their existence.

If we are willing to take an unbiased look, we will find that, in spite of all our problems and confusion, all our emotional and psychological ups and downs, there is something basically good about our existence as human beings. Unless we can discover that ground of goodness in our own lives, we cannot hope to improve the lives of others. If we are simply miserable and wretched beings, how can we possibly imagine, let alone realize, an enlightened society? (pp. 28–30)

Reflect and Dialogue

What images, words, or sentences in the readings most resonate with your life's experiences? In what ways do they connect with your life?

What is your daily practice so as to render yourself present to your neighbors and to God?

Describe a period in your life when everything seemed to "fall into place" for you.

What do you possess that you can offer to the world?

Closing

Conclude with one of the meditations on pages 55–56 or with a period of quiet reflection.

session six
VOICING OUR INNER "YES" TO GOD AND NEIGHBOR

OPENING REFLECTION

PSALM 40:7–9

> You do not ask for sacrifice and offerings,
> but an open ear.
> You do not ask for holocaust and victim.
> Instead, here am I.
> In the scroll of the book it stands written
> that I should do your will.
> My God, I delight in your law
> in the depth of my heart.

INTRODUCTION TO THE TEXTS

Merton borrowed Louis Massignion's intuition that we have within us a *pointe vierge*, a "virgin point" untouched by our sins. Merton extended the meaning of *pointe vierge* by describing it as "a point of pure truth, a point or spark which belongs entirely to God" (*Conjectures of A Guilty Bystander*, p. 158).

Who we truly are in our innermost beings is beyond the grasp of our self-knowledge. At the core of us we encounter a mystery, a "secret" implanted in us that knows God and is known to God. In the Islamic contemplative tradition our "secret" and "virgin point" is the heart-place where we voice our continuing "yes" to God because we realize that God voices a continuing "yes" to us. Everyone is sustained by God's love at the core of who they are, but probably only the most disciplined among us encounter their "virgin point" face-to-face.

This *pointe vierge* of God's image in us is the source of our ability to become nonviolent; it is the spark of our potential to become instruments of reconciliation; it is the wellspring of our hospitality to all beings. This inner reality, this bottom-line fact of "God's secret knowledge of myself in Him" is the basis for hope that, despite our fears, God finds in us a place for endless co-creativity where we are enabled to produce our poor life's share in the eternally good, the finally true, and the preciously beautiful.

MERTON'S VOICE
FROM *THOMAS MERTON IN ALASKA*

Sufism (a contemplative tradition of Islam) has some interesting things to say about who and what man is and about anthropology. Sufism divides man up in terms of his knowledge of God, his faculty for knowing God. For example, Sufism looks at man as a heart and a spirit and a secret, and the secret is the deepest part. The secret of man is God's secret; therefore, it is in God. My secret is God's innermost knowledge of me, which He alone possesses. It is God's secret knowledge of myself in Him, which is a beautiful concept. The heart is the faculty by which man knows God and therefore Sufism develops the heart.

. . . How does one know God in the heart? By praying in the heart. The Sufis have ways of learning to pray so that you are really praying in the heart, from the heart, not just saying words, not just thinking good thoughts or making intentions or acts of the will, but from the heart. This is a very ancient Biblical concept that is carried over from Jewish thought into monasticism.

It is the spirit that loves God, in Sufism. The spirit is almost the same word as the Biblical word "spirit" (*ruah*)—the breath of life. So man knows God with his heart, but loves God with his life. It is your living self that is an act of constant love for God and this innermost secret of man is that by which he contemplates God, it is the secret of man in God himself. . . .

The Sufis have this beautiful development of what this secret really is: it is the word "yes" or the act of "yes." It is the secret affirmation, which God places in my heart, a "yes" to Him. And that is God's secret. He knows my "yes" even when I am not saying it. My destiny in life—final integration—is to uncover this "yes" so that my life is totally and completely a "yes" to God, a complete assent to God. (pp. 53–54)

ANOTHER VOICE
COLEMAN BARKS, *THE SOUL OF RUMI*

"A SONG OF BEING EMPTY"

> A certain sufi tore his robe in grief, and the
> tearing brought such relief he gave
> the robe the name *faraji*, which means "ripped
> open," or "happiness," or "one who brings
> the joy of being opened." It comes from the
> stem *faraj*, which also refers to
> the genitals, male and female. His teacher understood the purity of the action,

while others just saw the ragged appearance.
If you want peace and purity, tear away your
coverings. This is the purpose of emotion, to let
a streaming beauty
flow through you. Call it spirit, elixir, or the
original agreement between yourself
and God. Opening into that gives peace, a song
of being empty, pure silence. (p. 141)

REFLECT AND DIALOGUE

What images, words, or sentences in the readings most resonate with your life's experiences? In what ways do they connect with your life?

What sense does it make to you that your deepest self is God's "secret"?

How would it affect your daily relationships if you understood that every being is a bearer of "God's secret"?

Where in your daily life are you realizing that "a streaming beauty flows through you"?

CLOSING

Conclude with one of the meditations on pages 55–56 or with a period of quiet reflection.

session seven

FINDING OUR PLACE IN GOD'S SCHEME OF THINGS

OPENING REFLECTION

PSALM 1:1–2

> Happy indeed is the man
> who follows not the counsel of the wicked;
> nor lingers in the way of sinners
> nor sits in the company of scorners,
> but whose delight is the law of the Lord
> and who ponders his law day and night.

INTRODUCTION TO THE TEXTS

Celebrating being alive is foundational for contemplative living. Our chief role in nature is celebration. For Merton a human being is "the place nature 'leaves open.'" Each human being therefore becomes "the conscious one, the one who is aware, who sees all as a unity, who offers it to God in praise, joy, and thanks."

Our present moments of awareness unite us with all creation so that our celebrating hearts transcend our particular time and even our own selves as we consciously unite our celebrations with all the praise that has been and will ever be. If there is a musical score to a contemplative life, its most beautiful songs are in the major keys of joy.

Merton's Voice
From *Conjectures of A Guilty Bystander*

A spring morning alone in the woods. Sunrise: the enormous yolk of energy spreading and spreading as if to take over the entire sky. After that: the ceremonies of the birds feeding in the wet grass. The meadowlark, feeding and singing. Then the quiet, totally silent, dry, sun-drenched mid-morning of spring, under the climbing sun. April is not the cruelest month, not in Kentucky. It was hard to say Psalms. Attention would get carried away in the vast blue arc of the sky, trees, hills, grass, and all things. How absolutely central is the truth that we are first of all part of nature, though we are a very special part, that which is conscious of God. In solitude, one is entirely surrounded by beings which perfectly obey God. This leaves only one place open for me, and if I occupy that place then I, too, am fulfilling His will. The place nature "leaves open" belongs to the conscious one, the one who is aware, who sees all as a unity, who offers it to God in praise, joy, thanks. To me, there are not "spiritual acts" or special virtues, but rather the simple, normal, obvious functions of man, without which it is hard to see how he can be human. Obviously he has learned to live in another dimension, that which one may call "the world" in the sense of a realm of man and his machines, in which each individual is closed in upon himself and his own ideas—clear or unclear—his own desires, his own concerns, and no one pays any attention to the whole. One has to be alone, under the sky, before everything falls into place and one finds his own place in the midst of it all.

It is not Christianity, far from it, that separates man from the cosmos, the world of sense and of nature. On the contrary, it is man's own technocratic and self-centered "worldliness" which is in reality a falsification and a perversion of natural perspectives, which separates him from the reality of creation, and enables him to act out his fantasies as a little autonomous god, seeing and judging everything in relation to himself.

We have to have the humility first of all to realize ourselves as part of nature. Denial of this results only in madnesses and cruelties. . . .

It was one good morning. A return in the spirit to the first morning of the world. (pp. 294–295)

ANOTHER VOICE
DOROTHEE SOELLE, *THE SILENT CRY*

Going even further back in time, trying by this circuitous route to get closer to the point, I refer to the Chinese mystic and philosopher who is believed to have lived during the fourth century B.C.E. and became known by the name of Lao-tzu, "the ancient master." He understood the ego to be "a gift on loan to us by the universe." What is on loan is not taken as a possession but as a temporary and care-filled and loving acceptance of something that connects us with others around, before, and after us. An ego on loan is at home in the cosmos rather differently than the one possessed as one's own; it can leave itself behind and weave itself into larger webs. "Go out of yourself and let yourself go" is the medieval version of this kind of freedom.

To be able to walk away from the ego fortified in possessiveness means to recognize what has been given as something on loan. By no longer having to be purely individual, the ego participates communally in the universe. The utterly unfathomable Tao, present before heaven and earth came to be, can be seen as the mother of the world or as the mother of ten thousand beings. In this sense, Tao, the impersonal deity, has also a personal side. Lao-tzu, who came from a region of matriarchal culture, uses the image of the mother but also speaks of the primordial father of all things. What is decisive is the relation to the primordial ground of the universe, for it is this relation that creates a kind of ego-lessness in the temporarily loaned ego.

There is a story about the great impressionist painter Claude Monet (1840–1926) that throws light on this different relation to the ego. On Monet's eightieth birthday, a photographer from Paris visited him, wanting to take pictures of him. But Monet said coolly, "Come back next spring and take pictures of my flowers in the garden, they look more like me than I do." A mystical answer! Becoming ego-less does not begin with the superego's demands or rituals of purification but in the amazing sharing of the one life that is in everything. (pp. 213–214)

Reflect and Dialogue

What images, words, or sentences in the readings most resonate with your life's experiences? In what ways do they connect with your life?

How has "celebration" become foundational to your spiritual life?

In what situations have you found yourself open to the present moment and to praising God?

Of what would you tell a photographer to take a picture because it looks "more like you than you do"?

Closing

Conclude with one of the meditations on pages 55–56 or with a period of quiet reflection.

session eight
DYING AS A CATALYST FOR CONTINUING TRANSFORMATION

OPENING REFLECTION

PSALM 40:2–4

> I waited, I waited for the Lord
> and he stooped down to me;
> he heard my cry.
>
> He drew me from the deadly pit,
> from the miry clay.
> He set my feet upon a rock
> and made my footsteps firm.
>
> He put a new song into my mouth,
> praise of our God.
> Many shall see and fear
> and shall trust in the Lord.

INTRODUCTION TO THE TEXTS

The central task of contemplative living is what Cistercian Abbot John Eudes Bamberger calls an "inner remaking of the heart." Our vocation is to become our truest, best and most beautiful selves. Merton told himself that he had "to be the person I am and to have the particular place and function I have, to be myself in the sense of choosing to tend toward what God wants me to be and to orient my whole life to being the person He loves."

A daily dying is the catalyst for personal relationships to God and neighbor (Martin Luther). Dying to what hampers our lives in communities keeps us evolving in the Spirit so that we leave behind what is good in order to embrace what is better and to act in ways that align our visions to God's vision, that we love one another.

MERTON'S VOICE
FROM DANCING IN THE WATER OF LIFE

I come here [to solitude in my hermitage] to die and love. I come here to be created by the Spirit in Christ.

I am called here to grow. "Death" is a critical point of growth, or transition to a new mode of being, to a maturity and fruitfulness that I do not know (they are in Christ and in His Kingdom). The child in the womb does not know what will come after birth. He must be born in order to live. I am here to learn to face death as my birth.

This solitude—a refuge under His wings, a place to hide myself in His Name, is therefore a sanctuary, where the grace of Baptism remains a conscious, living, active reality, valid not only for me but for the whole Church. Here, planted as a seed in the cosmos, I will be a Christ seed, and bring fruit for other men. Death and rising in Christ.

Need to be "confirmed" in vocation by the Spirit . . . This ordains me to be the person I am and to have the particular place and function I have, to be myself in the sense of choosing to tend toward what God wants me to be, and to orient my whole life to being the person He loves. (pp. 333–334)

Another Voice
John Eudes Bamberger, "Fragments for a Vision of Cistercian Life in the Twenty-first Century"

The dominant, ruling concept of my vision of Cistercian life for the twenty-first century is the monastery as a school of charity where all the essential, practical skills for attaining to union with God are acquired. Fidelity to this concept, taken directly from the tradition, engages us to present it in a more dynamic manner than was perhaps as necessary or as possible as is now the case. The first characteristic of this school that I would stress is that its program is ordered primarily to experience; knowledge, to be sure, must be imparted, and done so, as far as possible, profiting from the many valuable insights of the last decades of scholarly studies in the tradition. However, not only the final goal, which is union with God in the kingdom of heaven, but also the immediate aim, the *scopos*, as Cassian calls it, is practical. Both the lifestyle, that is the structures, the horarium (hours of prayer in common), and the various observances, are to be in the service of a process of lifelong transformation. This principle has not always been kept in view or even understood as fundamental for the contemplative life. In our history, even our recent history, the immediate purpose has been viewed variously as a life of penance for personal sins, of reparation for sins of the world, as a life of intercession for others, for instance.

As good and essential as these purposes are, they do not represent an adequate realization of the Cistercian spirituality imparted by the early Fathers. The perfection of love requires inner transformation of the inmost dispositions, even of the inner senses. We are to keep learning by listening to what the Spirit says through the Scriptures, the Fathers, and the signs of our times. "Without knowledge there is no wisdom" (Sir 3:25). At the same time this knowledge is to serve as a guide in the disposition of our time and energy; our manner and measure of relating to others, in short, all of our activities; as far as possible, are to be undertaken in light of the requirements of this inner remaking of the heart. This school takes the requirements and possibilities of charity as its living subject, convinced of the transformative power of divine love that enters only the pure of heart. St. Maximus the Confessor spoke of the present age initiated by the resurrection of the Lord as existing "for the realization of the mystical and ineffable deification of humanity" (*Ad Thalassium* 22). He adds elsewhere that the will "has yet to be wholly endowed with the Spirit by participation in the divine mysteries . . . For the Spirit . . . converts the willing will toward deification (*Ad Thalassium* 6).

Cistercian life will flourish in the measure that this dynamic conception effectively bears upon actual ascetical and contemplative practice. The concept and vocabulary of transformation is taken directly from the Pauline Epistles where the expression occurs five times. It is the spiritual analogue of evolution, the concept that dominates in biological and cosmic theory today. (pp. 126–128)

Reflect and Dialogue

What images, words, or sentences in the readings most resonate with your life's experiences? In what ways do they connect with your life?

How is this communal experience of contemplative dialogue affecting your spiritual life?

In what areas of your life do you feel called to make new choices that will instigate transformations in your spiritual life?

How have you come to terms with the necessity of dying in order to live in relationships with a deeper level of consciousness that your destiny is to "become love?"

Closing

Conclude with one of the meditations on pages 55–56 or with a period of quiet reflection.

Concluding Meditations

A.

Our ordinary waking life is a bare existence in which, most of the time, we seem to be absent from ourselves and from reality because we are involved in the vain preoccupations which dog the steps of every living man. But there are times when we seem suddenly to awake and discover the full meaning of our own present reality. Such discoveries are not capable of being contained in formulas or definitions. They are a matter of personal experience, of incommunicable intuition. In the light of such an experience it is easy to see the futility of all the trifles that occupy our minds. We recapture something of the calm and balance that ought always to be ours, and we understand that life is far too great a gift to be squandered on anything less than perfection.

Thomas Merton,
The Ascent to Truth, p. 10

B.

I am sitting under a sycamore by Tinker Creek. It is early spring, the day after I patted the puppy. I have come to the creek—the backyard stretch of the creek—in the middle of the day, to feel the delicate gathering of heat, real sun's heat, in the air, and to watch new water come down the creek. Don't expect more than this, and a mental ramble. I'm in the market for some present tense; I'm on the lookout, shopping around, more so every year. It's a seller's market—do you think I won't sell all that I have to buy it? Thomas Merton wrote, in a light passage in one of his Gethsemani journals: "Suggested emendation in the Lord's Prayer: Take out 'Thy Kingdom come' and substitute 'Give us time!'" But time is the one thing we have been given, and we have been given to time. Time gives us a whirl. We keep waking from a dream we can't recall, looking around in surprise, and lapsing back, for years on end. All I want to do is stay awake, keep my head up, prop my eyes open, with toothpicks, with trees.

Annie Dillard,
Pilgrim at Tinker Creek, pp. 86–87

C.

Our glory and our hope—We are the Body of Christ. Christ loves us and espouses us as His own flesh. Isn't that enough for us? But we do not really believe it. No! Be content, be content. We are the Body of Christ. We have found him, He has found us. We are in Him, He is in us. There is nothing further to look for, except the deepening of this life we already possess. Be content.

Thomas Merton,
A Search for Solitude, p. 70

SOURCES

The Readings from the Psalms are from *The Psalms: An Inclusive Language Version Based on the Grail Translation from the Hebrew*. Published through exclusive license agreement by G.I.A. Publications, Inc. Copyright © 1963, 1986 by The Grail (England).

FROM THOMAS MERTON

The Ascent to Truth. New York: Harcourt, Brace and Company, 1951.

The Asian Journal of Thomas Merton. Naomi Burton Stone, Brother Patrick Hart, and James Laughlin, eds. New York: New Directions, 1973.

"Blessed Are the Meek: The Christian Roots of Nonviolence." *Passion for Peace: The Social Essays*. William H. Shannon, ed. New York: Crossroad, 1995.

Conjectures of A Guilty Bystander. New York: Doubleday, 1966, 1989.

Dancing in the Water of Life. Journals, Vol. 5. Robert E. Daggy, ed. San Francisco: HarperSanFrancisco, 1998.

The Inner Experience. William H. Shannon, ed. San Francisco: HarperSanFrancisco, 2003.

"A Letter to Pablo Antonio Cuadra Concerning Giants." *Collected Poems*. New York: New Directions, 1977.

"Preface to the Argentine Edition of *The Complete Works of Thomas Merton*." *Honorable Reader*. Robert E. Daggy, ed. New York, Crossroad Publications, 1989.

"Preface to the Vietnamese edition of *No Man Is An Island*." *Honorable Reader*. Robert E. Daggy, ed. New York, Crossroad Publications, 1989.

A Search for Solitude. Journals, Vol. 3. Lawrence S. Cunningham, ed. San Francisco: HarperSanFrancisco, 1996.

Thomas Merton in Alaska: The Alaskan Conferences, Journals and Letters. Robert E. Daggy, ed. New York: New Directions, 1989.

Turning Toward the World. Journals, Vol. 4. Victor A. Kramer, ed. San Francisco: HarperSanFrancisco, 1997.

ANOTHER VOICE

Bamberger, O.C.S.O., John Eudes. "Fragments for a Vision of Cistercian Life in the Twenty-first Century." *A Monastic Vision for the Twenty-first Century.* Patrick Hart, O.C.S.O., ed. Kalamazoo, MI: Cistercian Publications, 2006.

Barks, Coleman. *The Soul of Rumi: A New Collection of Ecstatic Songs.* San Francisco: HarperSanFrancisco, 2001.

Day, Dorothy. *On Pilgrimage.* Grand Rapids, MI: William B. Eerdmans Publishing Company, 1999. [Originally published in 1948 by Catholic Worker Books].

Dillard, Annie. *Pilgrim at Tinker Creek.* New York: HarperCollins, 1974.

Easwaran, Ekanth. *Seeing with the Eyes of Love: On The Imitation of Christ.* Tomales, CA: The Nilgiri Press, 1991.

Gandhi, Mohandas. *Essential Writings.* John Dear, S.J., ed. Maryknoll, New York: Orbis Books, 2002.

Soelle, Dorothee. *The Silent Cry: Mysticism and Resistance.* Minneapolis: Fortress Press, 2001.

Stein, Edith. *The Mystery of Christmas.* Darlington, England: Carmelite Press, 1985.

Trungpa, Chögyam. *Shambhala: The Sacred Path of the Warrior*. Carolyn Rose Gimian, ed. Boston: Shambhala, 1988.

another voice

BIOGRAPHICAL SKETCHES

John Eudes Bamberger, O.C.S.O., was the fourth Abbot of Our Lady of the Genesee Abbey in Piffard, New York, for over thirty years. He is the author most recently of *Thomas Merton Prophet of Renewal*. He lives as a hermit on the grounds of his monastery.

Coleman Barks taught poetry and creative writing at the University of Georgia for thirty years. He is the author of numerous Rumi translations and has been a student of Sufism since 1977. His work with Rumi was the subject of an hour-long segment in Bill Moyers' *Language of Life* series on PBS.

Dorothy Day (1897–1980) founded the Catholic Worker movement with Peter Maurin. She has been described by one historian as "the most significant, interesting and influential person in the history of American Catholicism." Her autobiography *The Long Loneliness* was published in 1952. Her account of the Catholic Worker movement, *Loaves and Fishes*, was published in 1963.

Annie Dillard lives and teaches in Connecticut. She received the Pulitzer Prize for *Pilgrim at Tinker Creek* in 1975. Her other works include *Ticket for a Prayer Wheel*, *Holy the Firm*, and *An American Childhood*, an autobiography of her early years.

Eknath Eswaran (1911–1999) was a successful writer, lecturer and professor of English literature when he came to the United States on the Fulbright exchange program in 1959. Two years later he founded the Blue Mountain Center of Meditation in Berkeley, California. At the University of California, Berkeley, he taught what was probably the first credit course on the theory and practice of meditation to be offered at a major university in the West. He was prolific throughout his life in authoring books on meditation and spiritual practices within world contemplative traditions.

Mohandas Gandhi (1869–1948), the leader of the Indian independence movement, is one of the great teachers of the twentieth century. He defined the modern practice of nonviolence, wedding an ethic of love to a practical method of social struggle. Gandhi's teachings have inspired civil rights leaders such as Dr. Martin Luther King Jr., Steve Biko, Nelson Mandela and Aung San Suu Kyi. He is honored as the Father of the Nation in India.

Dorothee Soelle (1929–2003) studied philosophy, theology, and literature at the University of Cologne. She was a professor of theology at Union Theological Seminary in New York City from 1975 to 1987. Among her many influential writings are *Christ the Representative*, *Suffering*, *To Work and To Love*, and *Theology for Skeptics*.

Edith Stein (1891–1942) was an eminent philosopher, educator, and advocate for women. A Jewish convert, she became a Discalced Carmelite nun, Sister Teresa Benedicta of the Cross. She was arrested by the Nazis and died in Auschwitz during the Second World War.

Her writing in English translation includes *Essays on Woman*, *The Hidden Life*, and *Knowledge and Faith*.

Chögyam Trungpa (1940–1987) was a Buddhist meditation master, scholar, teacher, poet, and artist. He was a major figure in the dissemination of Tibetan Buddhism to the West, founding Vajradhatu and Naropa University. He established the Shambhala Training method.

The Merton Institute for Contemplative Living is an independent, non-profit organization whose mission and purpose is to awaken interest in contemplative living through the works of Thomas Merton and others, thereby promoting Merton's vision for a just, peaceful, and sustainable world.

Robert G. Toth served as the executive director of the Merton Institute for Contemplative Living from 1998 to 2009. He currently serves the institute as director of special initiatives.

Jonathan Montaldo has served as the associate director of the Merton Institute for Contemplative Living, director of the Thomas Merton Center, and president of the International Thomas Merton Society. He has edited or co-edited nine volumes of Merton's writing including *The Intimate Merton, Dialogues with Silence,* and *A Year with Thomas Merton.* He presents retreats internationally based on Merton's witness to contemplative living.